AF304436

Maher Asaad Baker

Sounds of the Sunny Island

ISBN Softcover: 978-3-384-42120-3

ISBN Hardback: 978-3-384-42121-0

ISBN E-Book: 978-3-384-42122-7

Cover image designed by Freepik

Contents

Introduction

Singapore is a city that has such a great blend of culture that can only be described through good music. Due to Singapores being multiethnic with Chinese, Malay, Indians and Eurasians music is an important way through which people of these cultures express their society and togetherness. Given the influences from the neighbouring countries as well as the links with the colonial powers of the Western world, Singapore presents a successful effort at one of the regional rhythms, which is Singapore's own tune.

Singapore is acknowledged today to have a modern musical culture that developed from its multicultural environment together with the country's function as a trading port. Previously in the fourteenth century, Singapore was a port city which later turned into a place of trading and immigration for the people of the Asian region. This produced a society that is Chinese, Malay, Indian and Eurasian with the Chinese identified with music and Opium, the Malays with music and festivals, and the Indians with music and rites.

Under British colonialism in the nineteenth-twentieth centuries the music of the region was also affected by European classical/popular music. The Singapore Symphony Orchestra for example was put in place as well as music education policies formulated. After the independence, the social programs were designed so as to define and preserve the culture of every ethnic group along with encouraging an inter-ethnic exchange of artistry. The result is a diverse and contemporary Music Industry whereby performers and musical groups are as committed to social integration as they are to aesthetics.

The Chinese emigrated to the region started shortly after Raffles a British trader established a post on the island in 1819. The majority of them were ordinary traders and labourers who brought Chinese folk songs and opera and musical instruments including the two-stringed bowed fiddle erhu to Japan. There was also the Peranakan or Straits-born Chinese who he said had interchangeably adopted the Malay and Chinese cultures and over into song and dance.

It is noteworthy, however, that the native Malays who were inhabitants of the island were already in place when the British arrived. Their music is accented in Arabic and Persian influences as Islam extended its influence in the Malay Archipelago from the 12th century onwards. Dikir barat and the zapin are forms of poetry, music and dance respectively which are still performed today as part of the Malay folk arts which includes gamelan ensembles.

In the later part of the 19th century, Indian migrants further enriched the cultural diversity in Singapore. They originated mostly from south India and they introduced classical music such as Carnatic music, dance such as Bharatanatyam and the Tabla drums. Other ethnic community settlers in Singapore included those from Sri Lanka, Bangladesh and north India.

The Eurasians who are of European and Asian descent are also present, albeit in less numbers. However, they have also helped to shape Singapore's musical palette by being the first to bring in Western pop and jazz styles while also keeping alive the Portuguese and Dutch folk influences.

This diversity is the strength of Singapore because it gives the opportunity to have artistic interactions between the ethnic groups. However, music also validates the culture and one's heritage. The culture and traditions that Singaporeans grew up with give them an indoctrination of their heritage despite the fast growth of new civilizations.

Music is thus performed during festivities such as Chinese New Year, Hari Raya Puasa, Deepavali, and the Eurasian Fiesta. It is associated with events such as the Malay wedding or the Chinese seventh-month Hungry Ghost Festival. Due to cultural diversity, most performances involve the use of multiple languages and different aspects of various cultures in one show.

The government encourages such cross cultural interaction through performances like concerts, music competitions and educational policies as a form of social inclusion. Chinese opera troops will perform with Indian classical dancers or Malay orchestra players. It is also noteworthy that Ukrainian ballerinas, Japanese drummers, and African American soul singers are also frequent participants in the lineups.

It also plays a very important role in the formation of bonds within the different ethnic strata of a particular region. They attend concert halls or stadium concerts and, on most occasions, they are organized in groups of families. While musicians have taken time and effort to form collectives in order to ensure that folk arts are kept alive, the entertainment business remains to expand. Participating in practices for competitions results in youths coming in contact with different cultures. Even equal stranger sings together during busking performances as well as others who have one language in common.

The reason is, that immigrants from various parts of the world have put up residence in Singapore and if not well managed the society could have been characterized by disharmony. But there is elegance in unity in diversity, where each community brings their notes, keys and beats together to make a national orchestra. Through understanding music, I would like to define how it becomes the voices of people and at the same time unites people in a multicultural way. The essence of the Singapore spirit is perhaps this, the ability to bring harmony where there is discord and the abundance of the musical culture of the country could not have best depicted this.

The Roots

Concerning Singapore music, it is significant to assume that Singapore music evolved from the melodic and rhythmic music of the ethnic people who inhabited the Singapore island for centuries. Singapore, being one of the most important trading centres of the world has been the place of residence of people of different cultures and origin belonging to South East Asia and other parts of the world. Musical histories of Singapore reveal the travelling of people across seas and the effects of the breaking waves on the shore society.

If we go to the following history, it is clear that people first settled in Singapore in the early 3rd century CE. For these groups of indigenous hunter-gatherers and fishermen, there were musical activities related to animist mysticism functions and assembly. They sang their music for generations, through some of the popular tribal rituals.

They also used music in relation to their religious healing trances, initiation rites, marriage ceremonies, funerals and harvest celebrations. It also had bamboo pipes and drums made from the monitor lizard skin that used tree stumps to create a call for the spirits. It was used mostly when people or the shaman himself or herself performed the trace dance and danced in a circle around the fire.

Tragically, there could be no documentation in relation to certain tunes and songs and for this reason, historians agreed that the music is in the pentatonic scale similar to other indigenous groups of southeast Asia. The rhythm and drum patterns could have been related to choral work songs that were used while out at sea fishing and sailing, paddling upstream on canoes and headhunting missions against an opponent's village. Tribal elders could also sing a particular story or myth along the string or percussion instrument in order to let the generations share the oral history.

While the tribes were murdering each other for territory and the right to kick the other one out of the territory, the musicality of the interpenetration between the two was also happening here. However, animist religions ceased to be practiced in the Indus Valley civilization due to Hindu and Buddhist influences entering the region with trade from India and China in the early century CE.

Singapore is situated in the central Malay Archipelago and for this reason, musical ideas can be taken in and out of Singapore from over the sea. As early as the seventh century CE, Indian, Chinese, Arabian and European traders engaged with the ports of many of the ancient kingdoms of Sumatra including Srivijaya in Palembang.

Another connection that the Malay world had with the other regions of musical culture was through the trials; music of India and China mixed with the animistic highland tribes of the Indochina peninsula. Such gong's chimes, xylophone, drums and even the bamboo flutes of the gamelan orchestras which are from

Java and Bali must have been taken in a 'katipo' leading to Riau and Riau archipelago to have an influence on the indigenous quarters before the formation of kingdoms like Singapura.

Similarly, the musical ideas from the upland ethnic areas like the Orang Asli of the Malay Peninsula exported or rather travelled south with traders who floated their boats along the River with the music. Of course, the flow was bidirectional since Malay folk songs and poetry from other developing sultanates also entered upstream.

From 1299 Singapore started transforming into a port settlement its music was influenced by both the higher and the lower classes from across the seas. Safeguarding indigenous rainforest cells as Hindu-Buddhist, Islamic,

Chinese and the final European, American, Peranakan, and Eurasian influenced local music.

In the beginning, there emerged the initial stages of the music developments in the region which could have relatively more values placed on the vocal and poetry. Myths, creation and other legends, love stories, historical and customary legislation, and religious beliefs were sung in verse, and sometimes: music was set to the simplest boat lute, two strings.

The vast majority of the fairy-tale information about the formation of Singapore surrounds the story of Sang Nila Utama, the king of the Palembang, Sumatra in the early half of the 13th century who was believed to have dubbed Singapore after he sighted a lion in the mainland. Its presence is still being perceived through the likes of Malaysia's folk theatre of Dikir barat where Malay poetry is recited in chorus while the silat martial arts and frame drums are performed.

Sung narrative forms survived to rhymed lullabies to babies, songs for children on manners and behaviour, or morals, and memorized epics in order to pass down history, songs of protest as well, if necessary. Likewise, there are fiddle folk songs in the Malay language and one such song is Dondang Sayang where there are elements of tease, deeper thinking and social criticism in a mock battle of wits between the sexes through poetry.

Other aural practices which developed the shared musical identity and rhythms for the

Malay peoples are the call to prayer (azan) while Islamisation continued through the established channels of the Malay trade networks in the Malay Archipelago. Sufi artists contributed songs including Ronggeng whereas female court performers introduced music from Arabia and India known as Machin. Night performances depicted Wayang theatre troupes that performed scene summaries from the Hindu epics with the use of gorgeously ornamented gendang drums and the Chinese oboe.

Like any other early musical culture, the emphasis was given to the songs; but some indigenous instruments were used for accompanying rhythm and melody. Music ancestors discovered by archaeologists in the boat-shaped lutes, flutes, xylophones as well as the jew harp found in Southeast Asia have shown this.

The drum is a fundamental or rudimental instrument that accompanies tribal ceremonies, rituals, dances, and martial arts as well as vocals. The Rebana frame drum remains a critical component of Islamic praises and cultural events to the current generation. These gong-like instruments were large and intricately carved with symbols on their surface with painters; they were incorporated into healing, trance dancing and ceremonies. Tupai barrel drum was coordinated and they used it as a logboat and also used it as a resonator. The bamboo slit drums also produced low tones to their slaps.

Bamboo, the world-renowned forest product, came into sight and sound through cultures, in pan pipes, nose flutes, blowing flutes as well as a set of Indonesian gamelan flutes. For natural percussion, there was the use of krakah seed shakers. It appears that conch shells were used to make sound, which was used for passing messages across water bodies. It originated from the celebration of the rice paddy irrigation, in Java; the instruments, Angklung bamboo rattle symbolized the member of society, as the various tubes all locked.

Some of the plucked and bowed strings were different from the Malay two-string boat lute as well as the spiked fiddle from North Borneo's sape. Even the woollen strings used in Orang Asli instruments symbolized overland trading links with China for example. The gambus lute with its origin from the Arabic region linked musical motifs with the diffusion of Islam.

The numerous locally manufactured aerophones, chordophones, membranophones, and idiophones employed in symmetrical traditional ensembles affiliated with predefined geographical location was a perfect pointer to the sharing of musical ideas, textural and formal content within the geographical body of the archipelago in question. Thus, by the time of the mutual influence, common or universal musical gene pool had already emerged.

Indian, Chinese, and Middle Eastern traders established ports and settlements in the 3rd century CE and those interactions brought a large number of religious, economic as well as artistic influences to the region. In our case, it would be logical to assume that Chinese traders introduced some aspects of imperial orchestral music. Imitation instruments of orchestras included; serunai like oboe, ney the end-blown flutes, gambus the plucked lute, rebec the spiked fiddle, yangqin the dulcimer and the drums. Indians have made impacts on the gamelan-style orchestras and introduced spiritual melodies in correlation with the Hindu and Buddhist religions.

Indigenous animist rituals began to transform and incorporate other performances as tribal and localized folk arts - a process called 'localization'. For example, the genres that claim to be Islamic such as Dikir barat and dangdut music interpenetrate with pre-Islamic Indigenous principal main puteri healing dance. Wayang Kulit shadow puppet theatre also emerged and sustained and localized external ideas into sensible community-directed forms that translated spiritual realms through music.

Similarly, the Chinese immigrants adopted the nuances, pitches, and instruments of regional Chinese styles and indigenous as well as imported drums engraved the tribal rhythm of the ensemble. The Peranakan groups played Chinese Malay music in love songs such as the Dondang Sayang which included Chinese melodic instruments and scales that were over Malayan/Javanese rhythms. New to the style were violin-type instruments in Eurasian dance music and the Iberian blend with the form being backed by the hand drum such as the gendang.

Therefore, the performing arts sustained communal formations as spiritual, economic and cultural dynamics promoted the creative circulation and borrowing across this region that was connected more through sea trade than political power. The common ground was music as an essential part of the social and ritual existence of coastal and inland societies as a means of passing on legends in sophisticated seaports of the ancient world such as old Singapura.

This interwoven heritage, this openness as a sign of assimilation, would prepare Singaporean music for future waves of globalization as modern history progressed. But the strong chords are still connected with indigenous music and its function – to find a way to express the essence of the togetherness.

The native people who have been living in Singapore before the British colonization which started in 1819 when Sir Stamford Raffles set up a trading post on the island were the Orang Laut Sea gypsies and the Orang Seletar who had their original form of music as well. However, with the coming of the Britons, a new phase of immigrants from China, India, Malaysia and other parts of the world was the cultural shock, and musically new styles of rhythms were opened to the island outpost.

The British wanted to impose Victorian British standards on the Crown Colony and to this end, encouraged the importation of Western classical music as a symbol of the upper class. The British introduced establishments such as the Singapore Philharmonic Society in 1902 followed by the SSO (Singapore Symphony Orchestra) that shifted the focus of musical listeners towards Western orchestral and operatic performances. Musical learning in school also focused on either class singing or the school brass bands, which commonly arranged pieces of British folk or military music. This helped cultivate in the students an understanding and realization of Western harmonies and forms.

Some of the western music instruments and music styles were brought into Uganda during the colonial period thus affecting the local music. This British passion for forming brass bands was passed to the formation of bands like the Singapore Fire Brigade Band, and the Straits Settlement Royal Artillery Band in the later part of the nineteenth and the early part of the twentieth centuries. Military marches and other forms of these became part of the brass selection as well as pop songs and movie tunes.

Classical orchestras were also founded; violins, cellos, clarinets flutes, etc also started, offering strings and wooden instruments to musicians and listeners Singaporeans were also employed to sing Western church music and play organs in churches where Western hymes were practiced. The natives were also taught elements of Western music including major/minor scales, harmony, and staff notation among others.

Such mediums as gramophone and radio broadcasting in the 1920s and 30s allowed the penetration of Western forms of popular music including jazz and rock and roll into Singapore. In these structures knowledge of not only the local instruments but also Western ones were small beginnings towards the incorporation of Western in local music as feelings of nationalism were beginning to come into play.

Those of Southeast Asian origin who moved to become immigrants in Singapore under

British rule also directly influenced the nature of music in Singapore by making their influence on the instruments and form of music from their respective home countries. These have interbred over the decade but have today remained as strains that one can readily identify.

The Chinese and the dialects that came in from the south brought the tuneful folk music on such instruments as guzheng zither, two-stringed fiddle known as erhu, and moon lute known in Chinese as yueqin. Other items that are from percussion consist of crash cymbals and gongs which are featured in lion dances and also in OPERA classes. New local music would be introduced by different Chinese scales and singing styles that would describe different dialect.

The Malay communities from the countries of Malaysia and Indonesia have 'brought over' the ritual cultural aspects of the Muslim religious practice and occasions and these include the Nobat court music for the Sultans or Zapin dance songs for the weddings and Dondang Sayang love songs. These were the gambus lute, rebana hand drums and gendang barrel drums. This was done with the help of pentatonic scales and that gave something special to it.

The Indians who went to America for immigration were a treasure of rich and varied musical culture which reflected brightly here. The communities of North India performed Sitar, tabla and the Harmonium organ for the Hindu temple music and songs and a few dance performances in Bollywood style. Folk music forms introduced Carnatic songs and the tambour – a drum and also bulbul tarang – a stringed instrument.

Such traditions were retained in a bid not to lose the group's cultural identity. However, such shows as cultural variety shows, concerts, events, radio deejaying crossing language barriers and the rising nationalism have enabled these communities to come together and sing. These are the characteristics of Singaporean music that can be observed thoroughly through their intricate interconnection and postmodern derivations.

Thus, though even during the formation of the early framework of Singapore it was colonized by the British Empire completely, the island was opened to immigration of Asians, starting from the Indian sub-continent to the Malay region. Their music has often been successful in taking culture and home along with the musical styles that they introduced became intermingled in the melting pot in very interesting ways. Sometimes it may possess an Arabic drum beat, but the lyrics are in Hokkien or Tamil and equally, there may be Western harmony but sung in Hokkien or Tamil. Out of this emergence came singing and music –Singaporean style singing and music, growing, rooted in tradition and now ready to groove.

Ethnic Melodies

The Chinese are also part of Singapore's cultural fabric they also have a music culture they also have been introduced to Singapore making a vivid tapestry of music in Singapore. The characteristic major dialects of the area include Hokkien, Teochew, Cantonese, Hainanese and Hakka, and all the above dialects have their unique forms of music with a certain level of survival regardless of growth and modernization which cause a tendency towards standardization.

Running through this tradition is the operatic form originating from China, fostered for generations in China and preserved when the immigrants from southern China arrived. It is in fact a unique combination of singing, dancing, performing and fighting in a style that is unique to the Chinese art form which is a style of Hokkien opera from Singapore, which is detailed and done in the Hokkien language. These themes are most often associated with a historical story or a martial arts story and the characters dressed appropriately for the good, for the truth or for the lie.

The singing in Teochew's opera is not as loud and wild as people might expect, the singers even read the lines most of the time. Beautiful clothes and songs tell about literary characters' psychological states and their moral dilemmas. : Cantonese opera contains aspects of both the play, with actors and dancers wearing soldiers' attire and fighting intensively; and musical display in Hainanese opera can be simple love and courage melodies of rustic Hainan.

Street opera, a dramatic art that used to be performed on open ground with a stage placed on the roadsides during Chinese festivals, has a very strong flavour of the various Chinese dialects. There is still humour to be had from Seventh Month Opera's Hungry Ghosts show, which is designed to entertain the spirits thought to roam the earth in the seventh lunar month. Also, there are puppet opera troupes that perform for people with different Chinese legends and they use relatively complicated glove puppets.

Besides opera, generations of individual dialect groups of the opera are allowed to perform their native instrumental music. The Singapore Hokkien rehearses a form of singing recitatives in melodious poems accompanied by Chinese strings and wind instruments as well in wedding and funeral events. Similarly, the flute causes vibration in the temple undertaking whereas the transverse flute gives energy to the lyrical songs.

Teochew music makes use of six stringing zither either to perform solo or accompanying harmonious lyrics in the continuation of continuing song fest that may take for days. These aspects become evident for the given songs since they have an open structure and make it possible to refer to events that may occur at the time of performing songs and involve the audience. Thus, when played. .. in the hands of the Chinese when holding the instrument in the vertical position, the tunes span from those which are slow and sad in nature to the quicker and triumphant ones when it is used in official ceremonies.

Thus, the music in the Cantonese style could be described as representative of the key principle, the strident power of the Guangdong province. In the military scenes of the musical, drums and gongs are used and for the ritual scenes, rhythmic backing by plucked lutes is there. Other constituents are wind and plucked instruments for timbre to accompany the folk song in Hakka and Hainan dialects.

This rather extensive but coherent range tends towards the hypothesis that Singaporean music reflects the possibility of territory for various Chinese groups to sustain themselves so as to maintain dialects and origins. However, amalgamation has obscured the dialects and art forms which were distinctly defined. Mandarin has also been associated with the displacement of regional Chinese languages and musical voices thus relegating them to the background.

However, where there is a revivalist movement to ensure that traditional arts and multiculturalism are sustained. It is also believed that cultural globalization actually poses a real threat of creating identity-less Singaporeans. The state has therefore ramped up on heritage activities for instance museums, festivals, and recognition of ICH to address performing arts such as Chinese opera. Supporting this Endeavour are various clan associations, and cultural groups based on the streets performing; engaging in different home dialect radio programs; as well as teaching children different music lessons to embrace their roots. Television has also featured talent search for the performers of increasingly scarce forms of dialects and arts in order to avoid getting switched off as the practitioners grow old.

It has also stepped up efforts to locate and document marginal arts such as puppet opera and folk receptive rituals, many of which have lost their scores and scripts. They are also reproducing traditional instruments that had been left in the dust. Younger generations of Singaporeans are also resurrecting their roots through reacquiring dialect tongues to converse with the elderly or to belt out opera to keep their family and community memories alive.

This phenomenon implies a rising awareness of the fact that an ethnically diverse country like Singapore needs cultural anchors of the historic communities in addition to the Singaporean identity. That is why supporting the heritage arts preserves the culture disrupted by globalization and allows Singaporeans to find their place in the history of their country. It also raises questions about the role that Singapore's economic success has played about the need to cultivate a love for its roots. In this way, Singaporeans are still rehearing the tunes of Chinese civilizational enlightenment that have been sung in Singapore for some time.

Dondang Sayang as the name suggests is an antique form of traditional Malay music aimed at the voicing of love and messages in the romantic context. It is a song that is mostly sung by a man and a woman, where they sing playfully, improvising on quatrains. The verses of the song are recited with the melody that is traditionally assigned to the piece and accompanied by the cylindrical Malay frame drum – rebana.

Dondang sayang pioneered itself in the 1930s in Singapore as one of the most famous arts connected with the Bangsawan, that is Malay opera. It was sung between acts or scenes of a Bangsawan performance by singers in the form of a singing duo. There was increased growth in dondang sayang after the post-war years as there was a change from being mostly a theatrical performance to a performance at weddings and other functions. It became popular in the 50s – 60s due to radio broadcasts. Nonetheless, over time, few original performers of dondang sayang remained, although attempts are being made at present to stage the unique tradition.

Regardless, the essence of dondang sayang has been sustained in modern Singaporean Malay pop songs and songs that portray affection. Occasionally, traditional rebana rhythm is also integrated into modern compositions as well.

Keroncong is said to have originated from the Portuguese fado and was introduced in Southeast Asia by the early Portuguese settlers and traders in the 16th century. It gradually developed through the process of acculturation of various forms of music including Malay and Javanese and Flamenco. By the end of the nineteenth century, a separate and distinctive Indonesian-Malay keroncong style had developed.

Keroncong was introduced in Singapore in the middle of the 20th century. This became the music of Malay community gatherings such as weddings, birthdays, meetings etc. The song's unique feature was an impressive caklempong or ukulele-like instrument accompanied by cello, flute and vocals. It has been noted that early keroncong songs had no vocal part, only the instruments being played, but later recordings included accompanying Malay, Indonesian and even English lyrics. This went a long way in expanding it base significantly.

However in the 1970s-80s, venues for keroncong were diminishing in Singapore due to the emergence of other genres of music such as pop yeh-yeh. But, some bands and fans continued to uphold it throughout the years. However, there is now a revival in Singapore where people are keen on the historical and cultural aspects of keroncong. Modern Singaporean compositions of keroncong with pop or jazz influences can also be heard.

Bangsawan, which means Malay opera or Malay theatre, was developed in the 19th century in the context of maritime Southeast Asia as the synthesized art form that incorporated the elements of Malay theatre conventions, Hindustani music, Persian storytelling of the One Thousand and One Nights and the elements of the western culture. They presented it in the form of music and dialogue and their presentation was underlined by the theatrical tradition.

In regard to Singapore, the Bangsawan can be noted to have embraced its golden period during the 1920s-1950s. Troupes entertained crowds in crude wooden structures that were called theatres and acted out stories from history or Hindu epics in the bangsawan style with large and colorful gestures, backdrops and conversations that were accompanied by synthesizers rather than violins and brass bands initially. Vocal prowess was important and the stars were singers/ musicians in their own right and selected the tunes for the songs.

But, the interest in Bangsawan started fading off shortly after independence. Challenges such as limited audience, and financial hardships were realized by practitioners. The art form was also considered by many as 'low culture'. However, even in the 1960s-70s there were still a few people like Sriwana who continued practicing the art. However, by the eighties, media programmes took over the televised media and cut short the further expansion of Bangsawan.

Currently, while retro-bangsawan singing is still a subject of fascination, existing theatre-based Malay opera has vanished from Singapore since the audience that already enjoyed it has died off and there are no new theatre-goers to be enthralled by the art. Realizing the inherent difficulties of living traditional art forms, organizations such as the National Arts Council of Zimbabwe are seeking ways how to make the young generation appreciate this history and give birth to contemporary offshoots.

Zapin is a type of performance music that originated from Arabic travels to Malaysia in the 19th century through migration. It is a dance for men and women, performing in pairs or in groups where the performers move in harmony with each other to the tune and rhythm of instruments such as gambus, accordion, violin, flute, and marwas.

In Singapore, the migrant Malay community zapin was introduced through stage performance during the 50s- 60s. It later developed and was taken as a tradition, particularly with reference to marriage and other festivities. The formation of more zapin clubs such as the Singapore Zapin Club, and Singapura Amalgamated Zapin Club where the competitive sites of the 80s to 90s were done mainly for paying homage to the maestros and for fundraising purposes. All these sociocultural activities provided continuity of the Malays' dance, musical skills, and language for the younger gens. The government also created some settings including Malay Village where zapin could be danced live.

Like in the instance of zapin clubs or the genuine form of this sort of music in which the dance has somewhat lost its allure to some extent, the modern version of this genre transforms into new perspectives and shapes – employing new gizmos which include new instruments or even the infused western dance-inspired zapin. Mainstream media also normally showcase zapin during the national day specials or talent broadcasting programs. Therefore the truth of the matter remains that no matter how much the ancient forms of traditional Malay musical arts have evolved through the three cosmopolitan cultural revolutions of Singapore they are somehow or the other saved. Thus, the state, in its attempts to preserve the identity of the intangible cultural heritage, is ready to introduce the young generations to the natives' origins as well as to new production.

Among the two types of classical music this one has evolved from the northern part of India and this is the reason it is referred to as the Hindustani classical music. Therefore it has very strong links with Hindu religion and spiritual practices that were in existence during the antiquity period. The other classical stream of music is Carnatic music which originated in the down part of India. The common instruments used in performing Hindustani classical are Sitar, Sarod, Bansuri or the bamboo flute, santoor, Sarangi and Tabla. They are equally important with the major vocal styles being the khayal, thumri and the ghazals.

Some of the earlier musicians and teachers coming from Hindustan who are settled in Singapore are Pandit Bhagwandas, Pt

Maharaj Singh, and Pt Ramlal Saptak. Present-day Sitar maestro Ustad Raees Khan is one of the prominent musicians of Hindustani music in Singapore present along with vocalists Kamini Prasad and Kartik Sundar. The major contributors to the growth of Hindustani music are the temples and other institutions including the Indian Fine Arts Society. other function givers comparable to the National Arts Council of Zimbabwe have also availed some support towards programs and performances.

It was first introduced in the USA by South Indian immigrants from Tamil Nadu, Karnataka and Kerala; however Carnatic music is actually very ancient. The following are the main instruments used here; the veena, the Violin, mridangam and gottuvadyam are used in playing the ragas. Singers who are well known are M S

Subbalakshmi and the young talents are Sudha Ragunathan and Aruna Sairam.

In the earlier stages, a few Carnatic musicians who performed in Singapore were SV Narasimhan, MN Rajam, MS Lavanya and R Thiagarajan but the current musicians are Dr Nirmala, Jayanthi and Kamala. Other programs include the December Temple Music Festivals as well as the June Temple Music Festivals which parade the talents of the year. The music heritage of Carnatic music has been disseminated systematically by helping Ayyanthole Sri Rama Dasa School of Carnatic Music and Carnatic music programme by the government-assisted SICCI have transmitted this music heritage systematically.

Some of the classical types of music have, in a way, maintained a closeness to the type of formality of performances; that is unlike the Indian folk music that has embraced the modern trends in Singapore. North Indian Punjabi Bhangra music is favorite among the India community and has most certainly fused with other types of music genres such as pop, hip hop and house. Punjabi folk song is a song popular among Punjabi culture and can be fused into other languages such as ska, reggae and rock by Indian local artistes like Oneroa Project band. During the multicultural shows, the Chingay usually has Chinese, Malays and Indians drummers, and other such folk instruments.

Most of the mainstream cultural support and staging of dance performances including Bharatnattyam which retains classical storytelling techniques are largely SG. The

Indian art forms have been given patronage for shows during multicultural fairs including Kalaa Utsavam. Performances and cultural fairs such as the Deepavali Bazaar held in Little India also include live performances of Indian folk singers and dancers of various classical and folk styles, which in a systematic manner hands over these performative traditions to the young Indian diaspora.

As an important aspect of Indian popular culture, the Bollywood music has brought about significant effects in the Indian music scene.

The most evident Indian musical influence in the international market and domestic market has without a doubt, been the Hindi film music from the Bollywood industry in India. Although it originated from classical and folk styles it has adopted modern pop trends such as disco, hip hop, reggae and electronic dance music. Bollywood hits are often on the list of Chinese language local radio stations and Singapore Indian DJs mix Bollywood remixes in nightclubs.

Such bands as The Artillery that perform Bollywood-style music are common in local events and concerts. Bollywood dances as talent contest segments involve Miss Singapore contestants of Indian origin as a tradition. Singapore radio stations such as 'B4U Top 10' and 'Bollywood Banghra' have special countdown shows that prove that most people in the country and immigrants really love Bollywood film music.

The Peranakans, also called the Straits Chinese or Baba-Nyonya are one of the significant ethnic groups in Singapore and Malaysia with origins from Chinese who migrated to the Malay Archipelago in the 15th and 16th centuries, and married local women. Due to intermarriages between Chinese and Malaysians over the years, a unique Malaysia Peranakan culture was depicted and seen in music. Peranakan music is a unique blend of the Chinese and Malay music and instruments, which were developed in Singapore and other places.

Most of the Peranakan songs sung were in both Chinese and Malay languages and a few songs included the erhu two-stringed fiddle and the gendang Malay drums. Some of the musical styles were dondang sayang which is a love song especially during weddings and the other one was joget lambak for merry-making. The fun facets of Peranakan celebrations therefore meant that there were many ways that music and dance could be employed in order to pass down this cultural gem to the future generations.

It is important at this stage to distinguish different aspects which determine the characteristics of the traditional Peranakan music and dancing. Used in conjunction with Malay rhythmic cycles and drumming, pentatonic scales of Chinese origin and melodic ornamentation. Chinese elements comprise ge di zha and erhu in Guzheng, other string and wind instruments while Malaysians engage framed drums, gong and some of the performances involve a violinist also known as a rebab player. Hence, lyrics might feature adjectives and phrases in the Malaysian national language and Hokkien, a Chinese dialect and even Baba Malay which is a creolized form of the two languages. This type of music is, therefore, communal as well as storytelling like the Chinese narrative music and the Malay bercerita music.

Interest in a culture that originated from the Peranakan culture was rejuvenated in the 1970s in Singapore and this opened up the floodgates for traditional forms including the don Deng sayang wedding ballad, joget lambak dance tunes and has brought about the modern renditions of peculiar compositions. Why in the twentieth century some of the classically trained Singaporean musicians and composers tried to compose new works which featured Chinese, Malay and Western elements and used Peranakan melodies and instruments for example, 'Straits Chinese Fantasy,' an orchestral suite by Kelly Tang which was played by Singapore Symphony Orchestra in year 2000.

Other fellow Singaporean musicians who have sought to unravel their Peranakan heritage in their compositions are Corrine May, The Opera Boys, and Dick Lee. May's hit single "Life Story" (2000) is a fictional one based on the family history from the Baba Nyonya perspective, which helped her garner her first set of fans. The Opera Boys were more contemporary in approach to their tunes with the album "Opera Joget" in 2021, which was more of a traditional party joget lambak song with a twist of pop vocals, drums and even electric guitar.

This has been a constant source of inspiration for Singapore's "grandfather of pop", Dick Lee, right from the early part of his work. The 1998 album called "Life Story" chronologically narrated the history of Singapore from Chinese immigrants to the present day and included its Peranakan-related songs. Lee goes on to adapting classic songs such as "Rasa Sayang" and "Chan Mali Chan" in works like the 2013 musical The Little Nyonya and more recent Mandarin Baba Nyonya songs on the Road of Grandmother: the 2021 hit "Grandmother's Road."

The approach to maintaining and developing Peranakan musical heritage for the benefit of the generations to come is based on the inclusion of the young generation to perform and listen to Peranakan music. The Peranakan performing arts like the dondang sayang are preserved and operated not only as performance arts but with the support of the community especially through the non-profit organization known as the Gunong Sayang Association. NUS Baba House, university student groups for example, ensure that Peranakan culture remains popular amongst students and universities, indicating youth interest.

Digital spaces also help traditional arts to reach out to young people in new forms. Peranakan sayang classics receive contemporary adaptations from young Singaporean artists on YouTube; Singaporean blogger Mr. Brown humorously imitates joget lambak dances using the TikTok format. Niche players like Singa provide traditional joget playlists to subscribers eager to reminisce about their Baba Nyonya heritage. Web-based cultural activities complement the physical communal engagements and schools to foster young viewers' understanding of Singapore's living Peranakan culture.

The Peranakan musical tradition significantly enunciates their existence as a collective entity that transcends eras and cultures in the Singaporean society. By performers interpreting and reproducing them for successive generations, the living spirit of Peranakan music also helps to perpetuate the spirit of survival, mixture and togetherness of the Peranakan people. By singing, we are still linked to the Baba Nyonya narrative that formed the Singaporean story of the past and became part of the present.

Popular Music Evolution

The music of Singapore up to the 1960s is basically rooted in traditional music, which included Chinese opera music, Malay folk songs and music, and Indian Bhajan music. Western classical music was also listened to by the upper classes of society that was educated under the colonial rule of the British.

Nevertheless, the reality of the musical scene began to evolve in the 1960s with the formation of recording studios, radio stations and local bands which began to perform Western pop/rock music.

EMI, Philips and Decca among other large-scale companies started putting down their regional offices and recording studio in Singapore in the early 1960s. This could have empowered local musicians for the first time to commercially produce and share music with the people in Singapore, Malaysia as well as other parts of Southeast Asia.

Of these, the most well-known musician that was developed locally was Zubir Said who composed songs that epitomized nationalism such as 'Majulah Singapura' and 'Semoga Bahagia' which are popular even today. Occasionally, Chinese orchestras with both Chinese and Western instruments were also established and even got the chance to perform on air with Rediffusion Singapore's radio station, SG54中文频道.

On the other hand, other local music companies including Panda Records and Ocean Butterflies came to the scene and started to issue compilation albums of the new English pop songs as well as some other songs which were sung by local artists. The guitar bands entertaining diners in Restaurants and Lounges were on the increase due to the need of the British military personnel who were in Singapore.

From the Cliff Richard & The Shadows era groups like the Straydgogs & Crescendos formed in the 60s and specialized in western rock, instrumental surf & pop. Most of them recently had a stint with clubs of the British armed forces such as Singapore Badminton Hall and the NS Officer's Club.

It is noteworthy that as soon as the Beatles were popular all over the world, the youths of Singapore started emulating the Beatles and dressing alike. Some of these were; The Quests which got a recording deal with EMI record label in 1964 and toured with another artist with such international status as the Beach Boys.

Some of the many groups of Pop-Rock of 1960 are The Crescendos, The Thunderbirds, Pastel Six, The Silver Strings, The Trailers and many more They were much more involved in depicting themselves through album art and having long hair which was quite rebellious for an oriental mind after thirty years of British colonization.

As a similar rate of success alongside Western pop, there were measures towards integrating the trends in international pop music with the locally prominent language and culture. Sakura Teng and Rita Chao popularised Chinese pop songs with sgEng (Singlish) to the mainstream society of Singapore.

Some artists like Fred Cheong took the British pop sounds and added Chinese orchestration hence giving him a difference from other English cover bands. Other local Indian group were a spin-off group of The Quests, The Young men played Tamil pop music to cater to the Indian market in South East Asia. Some of the local artists included Cliff Richard who was based in Singapore touring and also sang in Malay hence as you can see there were those in the audience who were Malay-speaking.

Hence, one could also think that the sixties laid a strong foundation for the growth of home-grown talent. The locals were just able to perfect their methods in the course of less than several years so that they could perform and give concerts and tours within equal status as the foreign artists. It also helped to meet public demand for the newest and most popular Western pop music and the early beginnings of Singapore to develop multicultural music as the country moved towards political independence in 1965.

The Malay pop music yeh-yeh was said to have reached its golden age during the 1960s-70s which was called the Golden Age of Pop Yeh-Yeh. In the case of Pop Yeh-Yeh, it would only be possible to qualify it as Singapore's equivalent of the Malay pop-rock that mixed Singapore's own music with that of Western music with the aid of electric guitars, drums and horns. There are few musicians who played a role in the evolution of Pop Yeh-Yeh into popular music with the aid of radio and the advent of television.

From the British Invasion in terms of influence by the Beatles in 1960s then many bands in Singapore pop Yeh-Yeh. The Singaporean groups such as The Quests and The Crescendos emulated the British bands and also adopted the recording instruments such as guitar bass and drums. There were other bands which mixed Malay music such as dangdut into their sound in the style of Pop Yeh-Yeh, which was the general style of the music of the period. Incidentally, the very name 'Pop Yeh-Yeh' is believed to have been derived from Beatles ' She Loves You Ya Ya Ya.

This was made famous by most of the early artists who were involved in the development of this kind of music including the legendary P. Ramlee. The 1960s was very early for an actor to shift to music and that was only possible by P. Ramlee who was already one of the biggest stars during the early sixties. His band The Silver Strings became more colorful with the incorporation of electric guitars and keyboards and composed and recorded songs which might not be like other pop songs at that time but still were popular, like 'Getaran Jiwa'. P. Ramlee is the first Pop Yeh-Yeh artist who laid the cornerstone for the subsequent artists to explore the adaptation of the Western component to Malay music in the future.

Another personality who partook in the formation of Pop Yeh-Yeh was A. Ramlie who was also from this movement. His band

Ramlie & The RebelsPubMed ID: inset;11073507 was among the earliest to use electric guitars bass and drums as the Western rock bands. A live band with Ramlie as its leader with a strong bass voice singing Rock with Malay rhythm and tune made songs like Bujang Selamat's usual sing-along songs. The success of Ramlie & The RebelsPubMed ID: The achievements of 11073507 led to the other Pop Yeh-Yeh groups to come out in the 1960s.

It was through the media especially the Radio that Pop Yeh-Yeh gained much-needed success and popularity. This talent contest by broadcasters like Radio Singapura, which later evolved into Radio Television Singapura (RTS), was able to present the groups like The Quests and The Crescendos to the audience during the 1960s. Since the major content of these programmes was schoolboys and other amateurs, these bands became greatly popular following radio appearances. They formalized some of the songs from the groups which they included as The Quests and The Crescendos, 'Shanty' and 'Mr Twister' respectively which became very popular and favorites for many people especially getting airplay very often.

It also expanded Pop Yeh-Yeh's audience reach thanks to the help of jukeboxes being one of the main purposes of Disco Parties. The clubs and nightspots in Singapore provided song requests of Pop Yeh-Yeh songs for their patrons and in doing so aided its marketability. Some bands proceeded to write songs that were to go on the jukebox and thus as they went round the clubs it had a beat to compel dancing.

Singapore's Cultural representation through media since independence in the year 1965. Local Pop Yeh-Yeh bands only were presented in programmes like "Pop Yeh Yeh" and "Kugiran Minggu Ini". They got a chance to take the last prospects to television so that 'they could perform for them', and thus got more fans. Local record companies including Pandaan Records wasted no time in allotting resources and signing bands like Jeffrydin to build Pop Yeh-Yeh into a money-making machine.

Other famous Pop Yeh-Yeh singers of Singapore included; Sakura Teng, Rafeah Buang and Broery Marantika Some of the synonyms of famous Pop Yeh-Yeh singers of Singapore are popular artists that were steadfast in entertaining the populace. 'Shelter band popularized songs such as Reach Out for the Love by singer and songwriter, Sakura

Teng. Rafeah Buang interacted with her followers with performances and such songs as "Sayang Semuanya Sudah Terlambat" on stage. In live performances once more people became fickle for the prominent vocal of the adorable Broery Marantika in "Juwita".

Music during the late seventies, pop Yeh Yeh began to be a little closer to rock n roll but had a small taste of the East. Such examples were Sweet Charity and the cosmoSynonyms for the cosmo-pop group The Stylers. Some of the songs include "Pulu Pulu" which is a Malay & English song fusing Malay pop and Malay rock with English dance-pop music. The Stylers were therefore able to capture the attention of many fans with orchestral soft rock ballads like "Hujan" which was evidently not part of the Pop Yeh-Yeh genre.

However, the first golden age of Pop Yeh-Yeh started fading away in the early 1980s as people started developing an interest in some other things. Although it was an achievement which represented Singapore music in the aspect of the developments of eastern and western harmony.

Xinyao, a new form of Mandarin popular music also emerged in Singapore in the early 1980s and it was to capture the emotions of a generation. Also known as new folk songs in Chinese, xinyao was started by youthful university students, singers like Liang Wern Fook, Billy Koh and Eric Moo amongst others. These singer-songwriters penned Love and identity literals, love relations, and Singapore Experience to march tunes accompanied by guitar. In the seventies, Singapore's music market was dominated by products such as Western pop music and mandopop coming from Taiwan and Hong Kong, but xinyao was in a class of its own and suited the young generation of Singapore. Thus, xinyao has served to awaken a generation that was in search of identity, an identity that has a place for the experiences of growing up in this new nation. This was as other elements of Singapore culture when under transition in the 1980s. Art forms such as novels, plays, and artworks that challenged and framed the Singaporean identity appeared when Singapore was in a state of transitioning into modernity. This led to the search for Identity and this was seen in music through the Xinyao music.

Xinyao was formulated in a university environment and the most well-known one was from the National University of Singapore abbreviated as NUS. Liang Wern Fook, another singer-songwriter also would compose songs and sing them in various campus productions, singing contests and the like. These songs were melodies with verses giving an emphasis on love, friends and social problems the folk-oriented songs were the kind of music that could captivate the student listeners who were always willing to listen to music that would matter to them.

Capitalizing on the campus fun, the xinyao phenomenon then gradually evolved and spread further afield, from the universities. Teo said that the late Billy Koh, an NUS Law student at the time, organized Singapore's first talent search event in 1980 called the Singapore Pop Song Writing Competition. This competition received more than 600 songs and some of the discovered talents include Eric Moo. back in the days New World Amusement Park and Golden Dome were some of the venues where the xinyao enthusiasts held sing-along nights which attracted thousands of youths.

After its release in 1981, the xinyao songs have been frequently used on radio and television stations all over the country. Liang also hit the trends in 1982 when he released his first album One Person One Story, it was a record-breaking one that sold 10000 copies in a month. The popular "Shui Hu Die," or "Water Chestnut Mirror" song rang across the entire nation. This means that Xinyao had moved to the mainstream.

The remarkable success of these early xinyao treasures motivated a lot of people to get their guitars and start writing. Indie labels launched xinyao cassettes that filled the stores selling records in the community. The members of Yao Sha, Tan Kah Beng and Billy Chia, rose to local fame in Indonesia following their appearance on the Singaporean talent show Star Search in the mid-1980s.

The principal leaders of the xinyao movement including Liang Wern Fook and Eric Moo successfully entered record labels such as EMI and Pony Canyon during the late 1980s. With improved technical qualities and a more professional tone, the commercial sound took over from the homey essence of standard campus xinyao.

In addition, Singapore's cultural values have shifted because young people now have shared references and pride in local icons that embody their goals in music.

Due to its background in amateur singing among Singapore's universities, xinyao made the culture of singing accessible to regular people. At present, xinyao classics make up the soundtrack for National Day Parades, school functions, and karaoke evenings for the Gen-X crowd; and this is so, despite the fact that these heart of the community songs continue to inspire the passions of both youth and seniors, years after their original production.

There is no doubt that Liang Wern Fook represents the whole xinyao movement if one were to choose one person. Known as Singapore's first singer-songwriter to emerge from home grown talent, he is the composer of popular National Day tunes such as 'Home' and 'Count on Me Singapore'.

Liang's introduction to stardom took place after he triumphed in the NUS talent competition in 1979 with the song 'Na Ge Xin' which translates to 'That Heart'. It started xinyao with its guitar melodies and services about an unseen lover. When Liang released his first record One Person One Story in 1982, he established his capability to reflect the voice of an entire generation.

Liang's music is quite carefully crafted and developed – the words convey a real portrait of human feelings and emotions, covering love, grief, and the power to hope once more. Young Singaporeans seem to relate to his lyrical themes, especially those who are either halting their student life for national service or starting their careers. But in addition, Liang creatively included social issues in his music. This made the simple singer-songwriter into a leader of Singapore's emerging cultural nationalism.

Singaporean pop giant Eric Moo is celebrated for his dreamy voice and the elaborate, rich lyrics found in his compositions. As an undergraduate in philosophy at NUS, Eric went on to write existential songs that included "A Time Too Late", which turned out to be popular all across campus.

Being intelligent and still somewhat empathetic, Eric's lyrics were completely academic in nature and yet they harmoniously juxtaposed with working-class storyteller Liang Wern Fook. Not as appropriate for radio broadcast as Liang's folk ballads, the xinyao numbers from Eric infused with jazz are cherished by those who love music in Singapore.

Eric was also involved in the popular xinyao band Yu Pian San Shi or "The Wanderers". As one-third of this folk-rock outfit, Eric was instrumental in creating timeless music such as the song "Shui" which means "Water" that is played on the air to this very day. With songwriting this sublime and vocals that are equally impressive, Eric Moo rightfully takes the title of being one of Singapore's chief musician-poets.

Rounding out the first trio of xinyao, the key figure in the early performance organization, was Billy Koh. During his time as a NUS law undergraduate, Billy organized the Singapore Pop Song Writing Competition which played a key role in revealing prominent songwriting talents.

In debate about the progress of xinyao, 'You at the Horizon' stands as one of his most listened-to Mandarin songs and he is both a guitarist and melodic composer. In addition, Billy played a role in important campus gigs and concerts that were very key in granting many young artists, singers, and songwriters breakthrough exposure.

He was essential in getting xinyao off the ground and turning it into a complete industry trend. After choosing to exit the spotlight and focus on AIDS/HIV non-profits and gay organizations, Billy's simple input formed the basis for xinyao to appeal to youth in Singapore wishing to sing about their feelings.

Even though xinyao is unmistakably labelled as a product of Singapore, it gained notoriety in various regions, particularly those places that speak Mandarin. It's not shocking that Taiwan identified with the genre, given the similarities between the university folk movement on the island and xinyao.

Eric Moo saw a great number of fans in Taiwan and China. Terms used by critics to describe his musicianship included 'Singaporean Jobim', in honour of Brazil's music legend Antonio Carlos Jobim.

The reason Indonesia took an active interest in the xinyao scene was mainly due to the considerable community of Chinese Indonesians living there. Lots of the Xinyao hits were the biggest hits in the 1980s broadcasts of Radio Indonesia, which used the Chinese language.

The attention from the region brought to our attention Singapore's growing Mandarin pop scene. For a long time neglected by major players like Taiwan and Hong Kong, xinyao declared that Singapore had made it onto the list of Chinese music giants generating hit songs. More ambitious performers abroad responded to the xinyao songwriting experience by bringing this aesthetic movement to their homeland.

In 1990, however, xinyao slowed down since the draft and the search for overseas education separated the university community that originated this movement. Eric Moo and artists of similar stature intentionally stepped away from public attention.

Singapore's artistic scene still resonates with the legacy of xinyao, even many years on since the genre's pinnacle. In representations of Singapore's childhood stories from that time, Xinyao songs are enduring symbols of favourite radio hits. Their success led to a comeback of xinyao in the early 2010s, and indie musicians including The Freshman gave the genre a try.

xinyao fundamentals have programmed the Singaporean music identity. The Adai, an English folk rock band, was influenced by it's organic singer-songwriter heritage led by singer-composer Amal Prasad. In Taiwan, a new generation of Mandopop artists also features themes of introspection in their slow songs, just like Stefanie Sun. Today's artists emerging from the 'Utatte' or our songs movement have absorbed the sophisticated influences of xinyao protester song writers, including Charlie Lim.

Singapore has risen to become a global pop culture-producing center that dispatches creative talents abroad. The essence of sincere, practically written songs about Singaporean life can be sensed in the music produced here. Acts created in calmer moments in university hostel rooms tell stories of this Lion City to emerging audiences at home and internationally. Thanks to Xinyao, Singaporeans were able to find poetry in everyday life and to set our development hardships to music.

In the first part of the 90s, young musicians created a local music style called 'Xinyao' that started to emerge. The Mandarin meaning of the term "Xinyao" means "Singaporean composed songs." These performers initiated their performance careers in universities and campuses before becoming mainstream.

The Xinyao songs concentrated on local themes, as a large percentage of the lyrics depicted the lives and dreams of local Singaporeans. There were gentle melodies, performed on either guitar or piano. The rise of demand for Chinese cultural products that were distinctively Chinese was personified by Xinyao. The maturation of culture occurred for Singapore as it began its pursuit of a place in the music industry.

During the mid-1990s when Xinyao was at its height, concerts presented by singer-songwriter Liang Wern Fook would pull in more than 10 000 fans. The success revealed that there was a very constructive undercurrent within Singaporeans to support local talent in the creation of original local music. The reason for this nationalistic reaction was largely owing to the impacts from Taiwan and Hong Kong, where the Mandopop industries were flourishing, thanks to artists such as Jay Chou. The liberalization of Chinese popular music contributed to improving the environment's conditions.

In harmony, Malays and Indians had also initiated their own local pop fusion communities synonymous with Xinyao. We saw a cultural revival in progress.

Singaporeans welcomed external trends as local talents came to light. In the 1990s, the peoples' ears echoed with Western pop, Korean, Hong Kong, Japanese and Taiwanese music. The market was led by American boy bands like Backstreet Boys, which were equally joined by rock groups like Guns N' Roses in gaining importance.

After its 1991 launch, MTV Asia began to display global music trends in every home. The imitation of karaoke patronizers often occurred with the regional VJ videos. Thanks to music programs like Channel V, fans enjoyed watching the music videos of current hits from throughout the world. To better promote Anglo-American and Asian releases, Warner, EMI and Sony BMG created local offices in Singapore.

At the end of the 90s, teens began to use the internet primarily for finding different music styles and enjoying music online. CD stores and eventually mp3 retailers got their hands on international singles at a much more rapid rate, thanks to better distribution, which came weeks following Western release dates.

During the 21st century so far, the global dissemination of Korean and Japanese pop culture began via export activities that worked to enhance soft power. During the 2000s, Hallyu made its mark in Singapore thanks primarily to the television dramas that encouraged awareness of K-pop groups including Baby Vox. Soon after this, the M-net music awards took place in Singapore each year along with appearances by trending K-Pop stars. Other styles likewise became more popular throughout this period, such as anime. In those days, the sales performance of J-pop releases wasn't terrible, leading to the formation of the Japanese music shop chain CD Rama.

The residents of Singapore turned to different international tracks, causing music producers and composers in Singapore to start exploring mixed languages and music styles in their productions.

Producer and composer Kenn C worked together with Taiwanese artists A-Mei, as well as Malaysian talent Zee Avi, to write songs in Mandopop and English.

Singapore Idol Taufik Batisah has introduced a light contemporary R&B flavour into Malay folk songs. Producer and composer Tat Tong, from Singapore, has blended Chinese orchestral elements with soft rock tracks made for artists local to Singapore. Jane Zhang, the Chinese-Canadian singer who took home the Grammy, worked alongside Singapore's Kenn C to incorporate soulful R&B vocal improvisation into her folk-pop from her native China.

In 1969, it was Dick Lee that brought the melodious touch of Mandarin folk to Singapore, combining English and Chinese lyrics with Asian pentatonic and Western harmony into his own unique Eurasian musical identity. With Singapore's globalization, producers found it easy to position different musical identities alongside each other, moving and overlapping them without the burden of purity. Born from a unique sound, Jazz has developed into a pure form of Singaporean music alongside other hybrid sounds influenced by the immigrant population. Separating race in music simply becomes a thing we once did.

The emergence of new trends was a result of such cross cultural mixes. Stefanie Sun's popular 2002 debut LP combined R&B with English soul and Mandarin melodies, launching sound that would become a model for the Mando-pop scene as it progressed. In the decades since the late Teresa Teng, Sun is the unique Singaporean singer to achieve pan-Asian pop icon status.

BuddhaBeatz combined Indian Bhangra drums and Chinese erhu violin into techno and house tunes that are played by club DJs in America, Germany and other countries but are unique to BuddhaBeatz's style.

When the Singapore government spent billions of dollars on international creative events in line with the Renaissance City Plan launched in 2000, Singapore established itself as the city of contrasts with references to the East and the West. International DJs such as Paul Van Dyke performed during giant events such as ZoukOut on the Siloso Beach, which is still reckoned as one of the biggest dance festivals in the world today.

Singapore grew from a cultural vacuum to a hub of Asian action that shook the global music industry. Government investment made Singapore city attractive with increased quality of life perception that attracts the foreign talent and investment. It also became possible for local artists to venture into the international market. Stefanie Sun sang at Golden Melody Awards in Taiwan, which is said to be the most prestigious award for Mandopop artists. Pianist Lang Lang signed with Deutsche Grammophon, while local violinist Vanessa Mae achieved overnight success with EMI Classics and topped the Western classical charts as a global prodigy. A five-member Indie rock band Electrico got a contract with Universal Music Japan and got to tour through the rock circuit of Tokyo.

The dynamic cross-cultural musicality which was Singapore music at the turn of the millennium was given a very progressive outlook. Whereas piracy was detrimental to the old business models, technology ensured that Singapore's sound went global.

Currently, Singapore Music experiences the trends as the technological advancement and social media influence deeply affect the discovery and distribution of music. As production techniques merge seamlessly, there will be no stopping Singapore from leading nomadic pop forms grounded on multiculturalism.

Classical and Experimental

Founded in 1979, the Singapore Symphony Orchestra (SSO) is the first professional orchestra in Singapore that has been developing nonstop. Origins lay with the amateur Singapore symphony orchestra that came into being right after the Second World War ended in 1945. The first performance by the SSO took place on 1st January 1979 at the Victoria Concert Hall, with Choo Hoey leading Brahms, Bartok and Tchaikovsky.

Created from nothing, the SSO first gave a performance with 26 players. This group has expanded its membership to more than one hundred members today, who represent over twenty nationalities. Opened in 2002, Esplanade – Theatres on the Bay is Singapore's national performing arts centre and the SSO is its leading tenant. With a seating capacity of 1800, the Concert Hall at the Esplanade is the current main performance space for Western classical music in Singapore.

The goal is to present quality orchestral music to residents of the region. More than one hundred performances happen each year including classics as well as pops. As well as organizing its own concerts, it regularly plays with international soloists and conductors. In the past 40 years, the SSO has held a variety of regional tours to places like Japan, Korea and China and several recording projects.

This has led to its being one of the most expert orchestras in Asia.

Singapore's music education in classical music became a key part of its culture from the 19th century forward, once it came under British rule. The pedagogy in musical education of schools and military units during colonial times helped shape a basic underlying support for the growth of classical music. At present, schools provide music education before tertiary studies, and since 2003, the National University of Singapore's Yong Siew Toh Conservatory has offered instruction that harkens back to traditional conservatories.

Changes in educational building design have paved the way for the start of many community orchestras and ensembles that engage any age and cultural demographic of adult amateur musicians. The work of the Braddell Heights Symphony Orchestra, Singapore Chamber Ensemble and the Philharmonic Winds has helped to make classical music easier for local audiences to appreciate. Independent tutors make good income by providing lessons to students who aren't going to school.

Alongside symphony orchestras and ensembles performing solely classical music, one finds groups that perform both overlapping genres and theatre music. As an example, this includes the T'ang Quartet as well as the Opera People. The framework provides a basis for which the relevance of the Western classical idiom increases for today's Asian audiences.

Over the last quarter century, the development of the local chamber ensemble activity has accelerated. Examples of ongoing performances are in tiny recital halls, namely , alongside larger venues including SSO Centre. Fans can appreciate the fullness and nuances of the lyrics, completely unimpeded by the leading musical arrangement. The vibe has become more ceremonial because of concerts that enable efficient communication with the audience.

The opera field recorded opera performances beginning in the 1840s during the time of colonization in Singapore's musical history. During the vast majority of the 20th century, modern professional Western opera performances were infrequent largely because of the costly production methods. The presentation of Opera was confined to movie representations and unskilled interpretations.

With its opening, the Esplanade now presents a professionally nurturing environment for staging opera. Though shorter compositions are played more regularly in performances resembling recitals, fully staged productions require a lot of commercial support. In the last 15 years, the SSO has staged Madame Butterfly, The Magic Flute, and Carmen, along with mostly sponsorship support. Still, Singapore is without a dedicated opera company, whereas cities of its scale, for example, Hong Kong, do have one. That said, the rising awareness provides a spark of encouragement that such a grand opera might develop sustainably and locally as we move into the future.

Opera People has presented both the Chinese opera 'Pang & Liu' in 2007 and an Indian opera 'Banyan Tree' in 2017, besides Western opera. The bilingual productions that combine Eastern narratives with Western operatic techniques support the construction of local novelty. This integration provides abundant possibilities to develop the core of the operatic art form within Asian parameters and to bring it up to date.

The beginnings of Singapore's experimental music can be found in the 1980s and 1990s during a period of dramatic economic growth for Singapore.

The new wave, punk, and industrial themes combined with a local flair influence The Oddfellows, as well as George Chua and The Verge. Within their own country, DJs like Peter Tan and Mano Frenzy have made ambient downtempo sounds resembling Mo wax and Warp records.

Characteristic of these pioneering sounds were tendencies such as openness to the accidental, using chance processes, and wittingly embracing happy accidents – or, if you will, the unfinished or raw. Singapore's cutting-edge performers have broken through the margins of musical traditions to expose entrance to chosen disobedience in a society focused on conformity.

In 2011, KittyWu Records appeared, rapidly becoming one of the best labels for unconventional music. In KittyWu's performance lineup, one could see a mix including dream-pop artist bbhugs and synth-rock astronaut Pastelpower, who both express and interpret avant-garde trends through a local Singaporean lens. Influential independent labels such as UDPPUT and Big

Sky Studio have made a point to localize global experimental connections by importing peripheral international artists alongside the export of Singaporean talent.

Just as convincing were other avenues like Hear No Archives, All Ears Music and SGX Vinyl, which supplied important imports of vinyl and cassettes from niche labels internationally for Singapore's novice experimental music supporters. The Analog Cottage is one of the new small recording studios that has opened, giving musicians and bands reasonable financial options for independent recording.

Other performances that were done in fertile spaces also promoted this flowering. Perform unrestricted from format constraints at open mic Downstairs Bar's Anything Goes nights.

Witness Mutant Mouth's synaesthetic visuals, strange soundscapes and performance art, or contemplate on The Substation's monthly noise improvisations ranging from minimalism to noisy skateboard screeches.

Music as a Social Commentary

One has come to understand that music, particularly song, occupies a key role in the creation of the nationalist imagination and in cultivating patriotism around the world. The National Day Parade (NDP) theme songs created each year since 1984 during Singapore's Independence Day festivities on the 9th of August are a reflection of this.

When Singapore started its independence in 1965 following the split from Malaysia, it stands to reason that those era's national songs stressed themes of independence, democracy, and a new beginning for Singapore, a multiethnic and multilingual nation. The early NDPs had the usual songs that were sung in a medley such as "Chan Mali Chan". Still, there swiftly developed a realization that a symbol was necessary to represent the ideals of the nation. The first NDP theme song, "Stand Up For Singapore", was adopted in 1984.

Wrote by Hugh Harrison, "Stand Up For Singapore" was quickly adopted by Singaporeans with its catchy tune and lyrics that encouraged people to seek racial understanding, democracy, fairness and justice. In addition, it quickly became an anchoring hymn for Singapore's nationhood as referred to by the national song. It leads members of every part of society towards these fundamental values and principles. As a result, music does trigger patriotic feelings stemming from 'invented traditions' and even creates a national identity, which unifies people in its name.

In days gone by, writing the songs for the subsequent NDP has been the obligation of renowned local artists and writers such as Hugh Harrison, Dick Lee, and Phoon Yew Tien. Their creations retained a basic relation with the first national anthem, though they started to grow as they formed new topics including altering socio-political agendas or the increase of Singapore.

As an example, the attractive song from 1992, "Di Sini Lahirnya Sebuah Cinta," has been proudly sung in the Malay language to commemorate Singapore as the nation for each race. Elsewhere, "Home" as composed by Dick Lee in 1998 took a relatively emotional approach by linking Singapore to ease and familiarity for Singaporeans. In addition, both sets of lyrics describing childhood destinations and traditions in Singapore created the image of Singapore's evolution into a country after reaching its independence.

In addition to We Will Get There (2002) and Reaching Out (2008), other NDP songs encouraged Singaporeans to face recessions and health dangers easily. They bolstered national pride by singing the merits of hard work, tenacity, unity and compassion along with various other things. Consequently, NDP songs served dual purposes: they strengthened national identity and also deepened the ties among citizens by alerting them to achievements and inspiring positive values of unity in the face of difficulties.

According to what was discussed, yet another trait of many NDP theme songs has been the merging of the official languages to support the development of a multilingual Singapore. In 2009, the catchy song "What Do You See" featured English lyrics, interspersed with phrases from the three other official languages: Mandarin, Malay and Tamil. In addition, some titles include language; Our Singapore (2011), Majulah Singapura (2012), One Singapore (2015), and We Are Singapore (2019).

These word distinctions reflect that language exists within the nation. Singapore's national identity is sufficiently diverse, they stress, to include mother tongue languages together with English and Singlish creole found in some lyrics, such as "We Will Get There." Singlish underlines, too, the concept of local control and Singaporean personality, illustrating that people of varied ethnic backgrounds utilize parallel phrases and expressions.

At the present time of Singapore's development, NDP theme songs maintain their transformation and continue to configure the nation. Since the 2000s, new productions show that beyond nods to Malay, Western or Chinese songs, there is a greater diversity.

The positive message and a vintage of global music appeal in 'Shine for Singapore' (2010) were expressions of Singapore positioning itself as a crucial global city. Some of the later ND songs have begun to feature other modern genres, including rock, pop and rap, that comprise young vocals, electronic instruments and rapid dance beats.

Reviewing the theme songs from Singapore's National Day parades over the past decades demonstrates that each one stands for an important achievement in Singapore's nation formation process. These improvements illustrate historical processes by which nation-states develop their priorities and how they see themselves, flowing from a need for survival to current ones.

Like time capsules, NDP melodies contain both literary memories and the distinctive musical and cultural features of different times. The basic themes, objectives, and participation of people in singing and performing national songs play a key role in nurturing pride in local social development and improvements vital to turning Singapore into a modern city-state.

Another example is that the Annual NDP theme songs in Singapore serve to socialize younger generations into national mythologies and beliefs about the history of Singapore – while also imparting ideological state meanings of important national 'events'. Songs, for example, elevate moments of togetherness, equality, survival, or even pioneering excellence, to remind the public of the approved Asian values that Singaporeans ought to aspire to if they want to advance as one society.

In addition, the singing of NDP songs strengthens bonds and unity within the people through this unparalleled approach to emotional mobilisation. Their communications inspire consideration of national topics and an emphasis on a communal objective linked to state goals and objectives. As a result, the theme songs of NDP promote national pride and patriotism by commending the nation's persistent victories and recognizing citizens as contributors to this process.

Bearing this in mind, acknowledging that National Day songs contribute importantly to Singaporean culture, particularly through feelings of national identity and patriotism, is worthwhile. The change of the songs from scarcely surviving to anthems that celebrate Singapore's regional victories reflects its amazing growth journey.

As a result, NDP songs have recast themselves into richly experiential rhetorical appeals comprising nostalgia, multiculturalism, social unity, and aspiration. They reflect the nation's spirit and emotionally appeal to Singaporeans through catchy melodies, patriotic lyrics and call and response interaction signifying 'Singapore'. Really, one could say that NDP theme songs are a musical log of important moments defining the evolution of a Singaporean identity.

Residents of Singapore from early Chinese, Malay and Indian backgrounds lived their lives with music in the 19th and 20th centuries. When these immigrants showed up in Singapore, they had with them folk songs that recounted their experiences of parting with their familiar environment and coming to Singapore. In those earlier days, songs from Hokkien and Teochew in China's south told tales of travelling across the ocean, of separation, and a yearning for profits in Nanyang (Southeast Asia). In addition, the Tamil Nadu folk songs showcased a like obsession with home, as those trying to create a better future away from their known environment.

During the early part of the twentieth century, Singapore, in its role as a British colony, heard a number of songs written by locals. Singapore's elites educated in English, including those who created the songs 'Singapore Town' (1927) and the 'National Anthem of Singapore' (1958), played an important role in crafting the economic future of Singapore and bringing people together with their unity message under British rule. Even so, creators on the left were using Western folk designs in the context of their anti-colonial campaigns. Maybe less renowned, Zubir Said composed 'Mamula

Moon' in 1954 with Malaysian folk song references to protest British levied taxes on Malaysian workers.

The Tumultuous 1960s-70s: This compilation consists of protest songs together with regional pop music.

In the politically unsteady years of its beginnings, Singapore saw songs beginning to show a more confrontational attitude against government policies. The patriotic tune "We Are Singapore," created in 1964, emerged during Singapore's membership and subsequent withdrawal from the Malaysian federation in 1963-65, even as the country regarded the breakup with sorrow. In the same vein, songs developed during that time blamed military conscription as a result of the required National Service from 1967.

Protests on campus and by the unions in the 1960-70s sought improved controls on free speech with the intent of bolstering their political influence. When these kinds of circumstances arose, singers shifted to delivering more indirect social comments instead of direct political ones. Singers including Kassim Masdor expressed the principle of Fast East adaptations of western folk music through representations of homelessness and yearning. Concretely, poetry musicized provided an opportunity for plural readings – Adrian Pang's "Sang Nila Utama" (1976) transforms a Malay folktale to talk about cultural loss.

As sources of fun and a way to momentarily evade their difficulties, bangsawan and Mandopop also became popular regional pop genres in the 1970s. In order to serve Chinese educated Singaporeans, some artists, among them Sakura Teng, chose to sing in Chinese. The songs seemed straightforward, but they articulated themes of transience, love, and loss that a lot of working class audiences could associate with.

The arrival of television and radio station mediacorp allowed light music to find fresh methods of expression in Singapore. Conversely, the rise in educational opportunities and English literacy has caused Dick Lee to spearhead locally produced English pop music. As such, Singapore pop was both familiar for its enduring use of folk motifs and engaging in delicate political critique about the stresses of 1980s Singapore. Artists shied away from direct assaults on their targets and instead employed humour and symbolism instead.

Back in 1982, the Mandarin hit song "Singapore Really Change Until Like That One Ah?" ridiculed bureaucratic slogans from the point of view of a taxi driver.

However there were also struggles with the government in censorship of music. In 1985 Chen Jia, a rock musician was prohibited from performing on the stage because he was arrested two times for marijuana. Two of his songs also had to be withdrawn from circulation because it was believed that they were in possession of drug solicitations. In response, Chen's new band "Made in Singapore" now wrote songs with more veiled political messages about authoritarianism. According to Chen: "I stopped making such lyrics after that, but music enabled me to continue expressing issues of concern."

Apart from plain censorship, many also complained about the Mandopop which emerged in the 1990s-2000s as commercialized products. However, there were still some musicals such as Flora and Fauna by Dick Lee in 1993 that continued voicing such commentary theatrically. Its songs were singing out the culture of Singapore society through the dreamt love of a Chinese Singaporean male and an imported Filipina bargirl.

With the help of YouTube and music sites that became prominent in the 2000s, distribution networks are becoming sources of independence from the establishment of Singapore musicians. Hear today artists like The Mellow Lellow, their fans are reading more thoughtful songs on mental health, value education, or even the acceptance of the LGBT community. While they can still experience hate speech and cyberviolence, such musicians can respond to the comments and threats rather than being mudslimed.

Moreover, original film scores for locally produced movies have emerged as a medium for passing social messages. According to Lee: "I attempt to seek out the Singapore sound...Music makes audiences quickly link what they watch on the screen with their own childhood memories."

Singapore, therefore, became an orderly city in the 1980s due to stability and prosperity, but there are latent conflicts between authoritarianism and grassroots civic activism. In this landscape, music remains to portray the fight for more visibility, diversity and voice. As education level rises and global integration increases, young Singaporeans also want credible cultural representation on climate change, inequality and discrimination matters that affect youths globally.

Chinese New Year, Hari Raya Puasa, Deepavali – all these are significant cultural and religious celebrations in Singapore. Music is especially important during these festive seasons because it determines the formation of various sounds that are characteristic of Singapore's multicultural population.

Chinese New Year is a celebration of the start of the lunar year according to the Chinese calendar. Before the celebrations, Chinese music videos with cheerful tunes play from shops, restaurants, and the loudspeakers installed in residences. Holidays such as Christmas and New Year come early as families adorn their houses with red and gold items to symbolize prosperity and luck in life.

In Chinese culture, the eve of Chinese New Year is spent with families having large meals together and much talking and laughing. Then, many return red packets containing money to the unmarried people as a sign of blessing them. Midnight is the time when firecrackers scatter and loud gongs from the beating of drums symbolize the beginning of a new year. Old people go to temples on New Year's Day with clouds of incense smoke and ask for health and luck as the music of erhus and dizis complements more elaborate performances of lion and dragon dances.

Streets stalls in Chinatown have open air stages where people perform 24/7 from Chinese opera to pop stars concerts. Modern sound systems blast out the latest Mandarin pop songs as people go around buying the decorations, as well as festive food items such as pineapple tarts and bak kwa or barbecued meat. From passionate mahjong sessions to boisterous yum cha meals, the talk and togetherness rise in volume during this week of rites and renewals when Singapore seems a tad more Chinese than before.

The Islamic feast of Eid al Fitr is celebrated at the end of a month of fasting during the daylight hours of Ramadan. Several days before Hari Raya, mosques announce the specific time of morning prayers using the Call to Prayer as Muslims wake up to start their Suhoor.

Bersanding is the last ceremony performed by Muslims on the eve of Hari Raya, in which people of the family meet to ask forgiveness and ask forgiveness among themselves.

That is why on the morning of Hari Raya day, families get up very early in the morning and join other people in praying the Eid prayers at their respective mosques. Subsequent house visits involve close and warm embraces as people warmly greet each other with "Selamat Hari Raya" as they enjoy foods such as beef rendang, lemang rice cakes and chendol desserts. Modern Malay songs are heard everywhere – in homes, shopping belt areas such as Geylang Serai, and even taxi rides. Following the celebrations, radio stations play Hari Raya songs non-stop with new songs and remixes adding to the spirited each year. As is typical of Singapore, the songs and sounds of Hari Raya may not be religiously inclined and embraces all in celebration.

Deepavali, the Festival of Lights symbolizing victory of light over darkness, brings out the best artwork with kolams made of rice powder, the bright oil lamps and Indian sweets.

As the days leading up to it progress, occasional showers of oil make the preparation of vadai and thosai, by street vendors, perfect with some Tamil film music in the background. Get togethers with friends and families become even more joyful and people wear ethnic like Sarees and Dhotis and exchange wishes as well as packets of murukku biscuits.

The jewellery shops turning into social platform which resonates lively conversations, greetings of 'Vanakkam!' and the loud crescendos of Bollywood songs. Besides lively music, one can even hear prayers being said or Sanskrit hymns being intoned as many Tamil Hindus bring offering to temples such as Sri Thendayuthapani, and Sri Vadapathira Kaliamman Temple to celebrate the festivity through loud poojas.

During Deepavali night, a special vegetarian meal is served with jalebi and ladoo commonly served as the last course. Before giving into excess during the feast, the elders light up oil lamps, while chanting for health and wealth. From outside the noise of neighbours firing firecrackers, bhangra songs, children's giggling and people's chit chat even at night are audible. For that evening, the sounds of Deepavali festivities make Little India an extension of the Indian subcontinent celebrating on Singapore soil.

Although the spoken dialects may vary with the Chinese, Malay and Indian Singaporeans, the sounds of festivity become a universal language that is understood by the Singaporeans irrespective of religious affiliations. The sounds of traditional instruments, prayers, sizzle pans and firecrackers in combination with modern songs and popular treats; These sound identifiers for each cultural season are extraordinary for Singapore.

But there is also a charming strangeness in the mirth, for there is nothing like this either in form or in matter. The Singaporean culture has always embraced the concept of creating stronger bonds between communities through food, fashion and music as was evident during these times. As much as people are different in color and religion, they all wait for such occasions as celebrations of culture as frameworks for embracing family and friends in all classes.

Despite the years, technological alterations bring concern about the disappearance of traditions while the sounds of Singaporean festivals remain strong. During festive seasons such as Chinese New Year, Hari Raya or Deepavali, the music comes back to signify an onward march between tradition and modernity as Singapore's multicultural society celebrates and assimilates all that is nostalgically traditional and innovatively progressive.

Music remains relevant in the unity and passing of culture in Singapore. Musical approaches have aided in preserving the unity and consistent development of folklore across the different ethnic groups in Singapore societies.

For instance, musical instruments are played during Taoist, Buddhist and Hindu ceremonies in Singapore. Fire dragon dance, Nine Emperor Gods and Thaipusam, the music and dance offerings to the gods during the Hungry Ghost Festival are rather grand. Folk stories, religious or creationist myths and epics are relayed and sung to individuals in the community and hammered into them at least once each year. Music is very important in the connection between the past and the present.

Music is also used by several ethnic groups in Singapore as a bond and the bearer of culture. Regarding Chinese culture, getai, singing, dancing and storytelling on the stage during the Hungry Ghost Festival is not only for entertainment but also for people to come together. All of the songs are about Chinese themes, or the songs are related to specific values. Indian mythology has been portrayed by the performing arts like Bharatnatyam dance with the accompaniment of Carnatic music.

At the very least, it creates harmony within a particular society starting from the basic stability of a group. During the celebration of festivity in their homes, Singaporeans enjoy singing folk songs in different languages. It also involves singing in mass choir for National Day parade rehearsals, where people of all singing abilities are combined. However, there are Singaporeans in recent years who have attempted to bring these classical arts back to life by offering free classes to the public.

However, despite the city state's progression into a post-industrial nation, there are fears that these music genres and the stories they tell are gradually being phased out. Therefore, new strategies have been oriented towards the support and sustenance of music practices and the policies and structures of folklore. As for the changes, some of them are the creation of NTBs as the primary state institution for the protection of cultural valuables and; the construction of new special architectural and construction complexes for cultural institutions. There are also provisions for special grants and funds for those who wish to save endangered crafts and music dialects. Presently, coverage of major festivals on national media always involves performances of ethnic music and dance citing that it helps in maintaining culture.

However, the role of the grassroots and community level is to conserve the musical tradition. It is crucial for Singaporeans to keep on performing Singaporean dialect street opera and transferring the lore through singing. There are opportunities to learn some of the less popular musical instruments like the erhu or to sing community songs. This has also made it easier for people to share traditions across different social media groups. It is therefore important that the initiatives that stem from the bottom up, targeted at participation, youth and innovation must be pursued in order to keep the cultural stories alive.

It is quite possible to forget these cultural aspects in a city state that is fast developing into a global city like Singapore and this is where we need to preserve our musical and storytelling traditions. However, if the organization provided adequate support together with the efforts of the community, music can also play a significant role in the people of Singapore and the preservation of each ethnicity's heritage. The beats, melodies, use of dialect and lyrics not only provide entertainment but also become a source of nostalgia for Singaporeans in terms of who they are and where they come from, thereby fostering ethnic Thus, the practice of folklore and its development preserve the culture and transform it into the image of a collective character.

The Future

In a way, Singapore has cultivated the music culture and is still expanding with more innovative prospects. From Xinyao, Singaporean music to the streaming generation: This presentation shows the world music of Singapore through a new creation of cultural values. Consequently, Singapore has transformed into a city that can effectively serve as a bridge between the Asian and Western pop music streams using technological advancement.

Operating in a multicultural environment, Singaporean music production has adopted the international approach which still reflects the country. Mandarin Pop and Korean Pop have thus gained their listeners among the speakers of Mandarin and English as Western EDM and Hip Hop has reached Singapore in the form of Singlish rap. The urge of wanting to dress up in fashion from all over the world is matched by the urge of wanting to listen to Singaporeans.

Other festivals such as Laneway and Baybeats provide a space for local and international artists to further develop the musical experience for the artists themselves and the audience. They also assist the local artists to develop friendships with foreign artists, hence promoting international relations.

Though technology has come in to alter the way we listen to music across the globe; streaming has also given Singapore artists a way to not only showcase themselves but also generate an income. Specifically, the information available about the audience and the state of the market allows singers and composers from the region to address the needs of modern consumers who are present on the Internet and social

The ability to gain fans from all over the world through YouTube, and more recently, Spotify gave a whole generation of bedroom producers the idea of uploading unique songs online. Singapore acts like Charlie Lim and Linying have found their audience through the net and have gained several millions of plays from around the world. As for music production, they exemplify the spirit of the Singaporean industrial culture – entrepreneurial and technologically driven, steering the local arts industry.

To this end, Singaporean artists interact with the listeners through various digital media platforms to establish what can appeal to listeners in the international market as well as the local market. Technological applications affect creativity in an attempt to modify the food to the preference of the local consumers as well as the music to appeal to the international market.

Most importantly, the growth of bedroom music from Singaporean artists has further diversified the musical pool of the country. Sharing own works on the Internet has a contrasting effect on specific genres, which has led to the increase of intensity of punk, metal, and jazz groups' performances. New media expands the repertoire of the Singapore music scene by introducing new styles, and new ways of how fans can engage with their favourite artists.

Singapore music has always been diverse but technology has intensified this fusion in the last decade. With technology today, it is almost normal that one can work with a person from another culture. As Singapore is slowly stepping up as a regional music hub, works with international artists that include local artists are becoming more frequent.

These attempts at fusion paint Singapore culture as a hybrid that embraces the global view but is proud of its cultural diversity as a nation. For example, the jazz ch The next one is pop songwriting with East Asian influences by singer Charlie Lim. He sings with a lot of comfort over the new Chinese rhythm and lays down rich modern music that enjoys a market across the entire continent.

Fusing the two music styles creates new possibilities that enrich Singapore music and increase its potential for growth. Evan Yo is a local Mandopop composer who has penned songs for Taiwanese artists like A Mei Chang and his pop-rocks tunes are patriotic but not overt.

Others have also played a key role in the marketing of Singapore music on the international stage through recorded collaborations. For this, his work with Dutch DJ Don Diablo on the funky future bass track "Better" earned him critical acclaim at

European music festivals. Singapore hip-hop had Shigga Shay's trap single with American rapper Schoolboy Q. Here is the chemistry of singer Charlie Lim with Canadian R&B artist Jayesslee in the representative and emotional piano ballad titled "Home."

These musical cross-over performances depict how Singapore acts as the middleman for these new hybrid grooves that have the possibility of going global. As Singapore moves forward toward its vision of becoming a Smart Nation, technology can deepen the experiences of cultural exchange in the growing music industry in the city.

The growth and development of Singapore's music industry are sustained by the following forces. Besides the fluidity in which local artists seamlessly infuse international styles with local nuances, Singaporean music has naturally and progressively developed into a multicultural form that defines and expands the nation's identity.

This fusion DNA will pave the way for more crossover projects similar to the first phase of crossover artistes like Gentle Bones, Jasmine Sokko and Taiwan's Linying. This is evident with how they incorporate both traditional Singaporean music and other music trends from around the globe.

As evidence of this approach, there are practicing artists who have ventured into new means of utilizing technology in an effort to effect privacy across physical space. Globalization in conjunction with technology literacy will foster more intercultural music collaborations. Supported by the online sharing culture and the Group's fan engagement, there are also other local talents in the niche that should also be given the same opportunity to grow and develop other thriving alt communities.

Underpinning it all is the country's cultural internationalism and its passion for technology which drives artistic innovation. Since the logistics ecosystem has nailed Singapore to be a city of entertainment by hosting more art events, the exchange relationship between local and international talents will influence the growth of future musical trends.

Thanks to globalization, artists who are not intimidated to explore new territories where popular culture meets contemporary art, the future is bright. Following the Singaporean spirit of genre bending, technology emancipates new age visionaries to create new cocktails.

Heritage Preserving

While Singapore has been economically prosperous and is increasingly becoming more modern, there is a chance of losing the roots and identity of art and culture such as Singapore's musical instruments. With arts ranging from Chinese opera and Malay folk songs, to Indian classical music and Singaporean music genres of ethnic groups, Singapore's music culture is slowly struggling to find its identity as globalized popular culture threatens to dilute active involvement.

Western music and Korean and Japanese pop culture dominate the interest of the youth much more than Chinese opera and Malay folk songs. There are some types of musical art that have had their performances mainly in the past and only exist in almost extinction today such as the Bangsawan theatrical performances. Other genres are sustained primarily by the elderly, which leads to concerns over the extinction of cultural demise if traditions cannot be effectively transferred to uninterested youth engrossed in internet socializing, imported entertainment, and mass consumerist culture.

However, the lack of time and money for the preservation of music is also caused by economic factors. For the lower income earners in Singapore, it becomes a luxury to practice musical instruments or perform in theatres and concert halls because they have to meet other basic needs in life. For example, even the state funded organizations which are supposed to promote heritage through the arts face challenges in their funding even when compared to other sectors such as business and technology which are deemed more important in the growth of the national economy. Rent prices have gone up significantly in present day Singapore and it has become nearly impossible for the performers of historical musicals to secure spaces for artists, musical theatres, concert venues and rehearsal studios.

Modernization is also a threat that jeopardizes the elimination of cultural contexts and languages associated with traditional classic works of art in one way or the other. For example, there are languages and dialects of Chinese opera that not only encompass the music part of it but also include poetry and even the storytelling of the Chinese opera as a whole. While today the people of China and Singapore speak Mandarin and English, the Chinese dialects are almost invisible in the younger generations of Chinese Singaporeans, and the nuances that the masters of Opera It does so in a way that makes the already complex old opera scripts even more difficult to learn for new learners who may help sustain the art forms In the same manner, there is also a worrying trend of dying dialects related to Malay, Indian and Peranakan heritage musical art forms as well.

In light of the diminishing musician traditional practices, Singapore has embarked on several practices of deliberately archiving and passing on previous cultural practices to the generations to come. Such efforts seek to establish that musical art forms must be capable of staying relevant amid the modernization processes.

National Arts Council, a government affiliated body often offers grants and funds for research and education initiatives by traditional arts performers and cultural organizations. In some schools, pilot projects that aim to introduce traditional instruments and performance skills during music periods that are popular with Western instruments such as pianos and guitars have been implemented. The Singapore Chinese Orchestra also conducts outreach programs which seek to popularize Chinese instrumental music among the younger generation and players through the use of popular singers to rearrange old songs in more contemporary styles.

However, one of the most significant measures happens through careful documentation and recording of the remaining and scarce valuable historical knowledge on fading arts. For example, virtuoso musicians who are national living treasures document their creative processes and life histories in oral history interviews. Renowned Chinese Opera masters also pass on specific culture to new members known as successors of unique arts. Archives also contain examples of musicians or theatrical forms that are getting close to extinction after most of the great performers are gone.

The new generation and economic factors, the loss of the original cultural contexts, and the phasing out of the languages in which traditional music was stored are a threat to modernization. Measures to address this trend have involved putting enough funds towards the arts and music as well as progressing to other forms. It has to be noted that some information, which is culturally significant, is not always transmitted from one generation to another, and archiving also has to document such knowledge and performance documentation for the purpose of imparting knowledge to a larger number of people and motivating them. To this end, Singapore ensures that heritage does not fade away and thus makes the world understand that there is more to music as depicted by the global pop culture.

To set the context on the changes that have taken place in the policies on music education it would be relevant to start with the problems faced by Singapore immediately after it became an independent nation in 1965. Economic growth and development of English as a national language became the most crucial requirements of the nation. When the government started a policy of centralization of the public school system in the late 1970's the number of vernacular schools and therefore the performance of mother tongue artistic practices decreased. In this process, music education was geared less than the academic curricula and other core learning domains.

The students started to lose interest in their traditional music and culture in the 1990s due to the introduction of another form of modern music and popular culture. However, this decade was different as the music of Singapore was starting to be documented as part of the nation's history. The National Arts Council of Zimbabwe was established in 1991 to support the arts and its development in relation to the provision of resources. During the 2000s, the international community focused its attention on the conservation of intangible cultural heritage, and Singapore joined the UNESCO conventions to promote cultural assets through educational and archival measures.

As a result, the Singapore government has shifted its focus on arts development and music education accessibility in the last two decades. In the first program, a focus was placed on Western classical and band, but as the years have gone by, more world music has been incorporated into the program in an effort to expose students to the diverse population in Canada. Current national curriculum also, reflects a more holistic approach towards music in teaching and learning that includes listening, performing, historical and cultural aspects of music. The mentioned pedagogical developments together with the community arts projects are promising in action.

As a general context, it may be useful to discuss music programmes available in the secondary public schools in Singapore before turning to certain preservation initiatives. Over the past four decades, music has been offered as a subject that students can take to be examined during the final year O' Level exams. First of all, students could choose to direct their efforts to higher music or art since they are to take an art course. After the year 2000, the following are the roles of public secondary schools in music education.

In mainstream secondary schools, the basic arts modules give the student a basic understanding of musical concepts and practice. They explore singing, playing simple melodic instruments including the xylophone or recorder, and understanding music symbols. The syllabus contains the essentials of Chinese, Malay and Indian music and some exposure to Western orchestras. The first level is the entry knowledge which does not enhance the acquisition of competencies greatly. Those who would like to pursue music as a formal course may choose formal electives.

Higher level music programs require students to audition based on their previous private lessons or talent. Music majors take advanced music theory, more ensemble classes with band instruments or world percussion and either classical Western or world music. It also has the Performing Arts (SPA) secondary schools for young talents who give similar pieces of training as what is given in conservatories. At the end of year 10, the body of students preparing for important examinations that decide their future academic paths will be familiar with Singapore's multiculturalism and/or have some level of music literacy depending on the school music programs they attend.

In Singapore, junior colleges, polytechnics or universities provide people with an opportunity to develop their musical talents and skills for fun or for getting paid. But at this stage, the majority of the students who are not interested in arts related careers do not attend lessons or performance groups. Hence, basic engagement and skills that are learnt during the early stages of school during adolescence determine future musical experience.

To the people who are very much concerned with the proper development of musical appreciation, education in Singapore's tertiary institutions has provisions that are in harmony with the Ministry of Education's expanded arts and cultural agenda that was introduced in the year 2000. The number of music departments in universities has been created in the past fifteen years when similar departments have been established only in some polytechnics. The Nanyang Technological University founded the first art, design and media school in Singapore in 2005 and offered bachelor's degrees in music. NUS and Yong Siew Toh Conservatory then established an arts and social sciences faculty in 2006 that has since introduced music as a course of study with theory, history and cultural aspects of music in different societies. Examples include percussion, Chinese Orchestra, and Indian; disciplines even have a chance to perform in ensembles across faculties.

This third level entry, from leisure to professional level, results in graduates who are able to enhance Singapore's music and art culture. All of these are musicians, educators, event planners, and administrators fostering the culture of appreciative society.

However, as music is also integrated into the country's system of education, the preservation of art alone is a special process that involves the collection, documentation, and transfer of information to future generations. It was in the 1990s that Singapore understood this and developed centres for the conservation of perfuming arts along with better post secondary education. Two organizations that have had an impact on the preservation work include the National Arts Council (NAC) and National Heritage Board (NHB).

NAC has always backed conventional arts groups/programmes only. Some of these are funded by the government and include the Chinese Opera Institute, Bhaskar Arts Academy for Indian Classical Music and dance, Sri Warisan Som Said Performing Arts for Malay Dance and The grant funding enables transmission through classes, performance and cultural exchange.

On the same note, the NHB has developed archives, networks, and scholarship in relation to Intangible Cultural Heritage. Structures like the Circle of Arts aid in generating a list of traditional artists and groups that schools can use in their programme design. As part of the NHB scholarships, talents are also developed through sponsoring those young talents to be mentored by the senior masters. They actually function as a musical literature and construction of instruments library of nearly endangered species.

Over the past few years, these national bodies have shifted their attention to engaging with communities and schools in the heartland to foster an appreciation for cultural assets in neighbourhoods. Through outreach activities, students and residents are able to understand the position and history of different art forms in Singapore City. Practical and interactive sessions include learning Malay frame drum making, singing a part of a Hokkien opera scene or recording Indian dance movements all these measures contribute to the social integration of living heritage as generation after generation participates in the celebrations.

Thus, national agencies have established entry points, but it is education policies and curricular decisions that determine how certain music traditions are taught in classrooms. Here, several projects initiated by ambitious educators offer valuable examples for future courses of action. These experimental approaches reveal fresh visions for teaching art as a learning tool and for employing multimedia to help young people apprentice with old ones.

Pilot secondary schools have tried arts integration models where multimedia arts content area is used in enhancing other areas of learning than the conventional systems. Crescent Girls School for instance introduced semester long experiential learning programs in the year 2009 with activities that run for a semester and included things like field trips, crafts, and performances based on themes like 'Kampong' culture or Chinese minorities. Many cultural values were gained by students as they learnt music and dance lessons. They also did other tasks on other sociological issues to demonstrate the connection of the subject and the use of the knowledge. In the beginning, it was used for high achievers only, but in the future, it can be developed for other students. The infusion pilots show that students may be interested.

Other schools have elaborated on focalized practices with regard to particular cultural objects. In 2012, Malay arts in Jurong Secondary was developed through the Ghazal Song Poem Recitals and the Angklung Shake Chime which originated from Indonesia and early Singapore kampong. These classes contributed to the diversification of the campus given that Malay and Chinese students learned about musical awareness thereby enhancing their coexistence. Creating cultural programs in each school may help build the school's identity and also help to save the community arts.

Therefore, the integration of technology also has the possibility to solve the problems of practical limitations in the transmission of traditions. The pilots led by the NUS researchers used mobile applications and game mechanics to enable the senior instructors to control the junior orchestra players. The result showed that the apps could offer playing technique feedback; however, live tutoring was still critical.

Due to the cultural diversity and relatively small geographical area of Singapore, musical heritage and its understanding are taught in the framework of the national education system to avoid issues regarding the representation of certain ethnic groups. The early years set the tone of preparation, familiarizing youths on the diversity of the world. It is critical that secondary school electives are specialized and that tertiary programs maintain world class training feeders. The formal ones foster practical experience enshrined in practice, along with equal cultural orientation to make students understand other traditional styles apart from their own.

The reviewed initiatives show that musical appreciation coupled with personal reflection fosters intercultural understanding when continued from youth to emerging adulthood. Culture bearers rely on Singapore's institutional processes to ensure that diverse arts remain relevant to subsequent generations. However, schools cannot bear the mission alone. Grassroots arts companies and NAC-NHB programs introduce schools and professional artists to local communities that embody living cultures. All elements must harmonize.

Individuals motivated to take music forward from everyday listening into scholarly or performance use follow distinct arts education tracks. A few pursue academic careers in order to shed light on cultural concerns through ethnomusicology scholarship forming world views. These contributors whether operating locally in Singapore or regionally reinforce Singapore as a cultural powerhouse of immense diversity. It mainly originates from their early musical experiences in school settings.

In order to build on cultural knowledge and responsibility, Singapore needs to continuously work on the importance of arts in Singapore and as a need to safely guard against disruption technologies. Low also

All in all, integrative learning involves the use of both the left and right sides of the brain. It will foster the growth of more balanced and empathical, multilateral approach thinkers. Policymakers should focus more on positives of arts and discuss them more while the administrators should provide enough time and resources and the faculty should support them. All these decisions greatly affect the continuity of culture.

Creative learning activities such as dancing, debating or composition are suitable for the learners who may be deemed as exceptional or otherwise called special. The students should work on new projects that combine old and new in their school work. For the sake of modernity, there is a need for organic cultural progression, which is appropriate for Singapore as a progressive nation.

Popular school programs include the ability to foster student interest in various arts – from a Ukulele Chinese Orchestra to a Malay string ensemble with influences from the Ghazal poetry. As is seen once youth find other personal relationships with their families to enhance the consciousness of musical heritage. Finally, in order to maintain a living heritage, one has to move people, which is impossible just by focusing on tangible aspects, be it training new generations of artisans or creating documentation. Some of the key challenges include social justice, Equity, Democratic Reform, Sustainability, and Encouraging youths to embrace positive and role model figures as influential cultural pillars in the face of challenging 21st century realities.

Disclaimer

Everything shared in this book should be considered as educational and informative in nature. The author and publisher shall not be responsible for any loss or damage suffered by any reader directly or indirectly through reading of, reliance on, and use of information that only the author and the publisher know at the time of writing this book.

Some of the suggestions given and the approaches recommended in the book may not be applicable to certain circumstances. The author and the publisher shall not be held responsible for any damages caused as a direct result of the use or non-use of the information presented in this book.

It is understood that readers should not rely on it for professional solicitations such as medical, legal, financial, and other related opinions. If any professional help is needed, then advice of a competent professional person should be taken.

The author and the publisher will not be held responsible for direct, indirect, special, or consequential damages or any other costs whatsoever arising from the use of the information present herein in this book.

About the Author

Maher Asaad Baker (In Arabic: ماهر أسعد بكر), is a Syrian musician, author, journalist, VFX & graphic artist, and director. He was born in Damascus in 1977. He grew up with a dream of being one of the most well-known artists in the world, and he has been working hard to achieve it ever since.

He started his career in 1997 when he was only 20 years old. He had a passion for technology and media, and he taught himself how to develop applications and websites. He also explored various types of media-creating paths, such as music production, graphic design, video editing, animation, and filmmaking. He was not satisfied with just being a consumer of media; he wanted to be a creator of media.

Reading was another source of inspiration for him. He was always surrounded by books as a child, thanks to his father's extensive library. He read books from different genres, topics, and perspectives. He read books for knowledge, for wisdom, for entertainment, for enlightenment. Reading stimulated his imagination and curiosity. Reading also developed his writing skills.

He did not start writing professionally until later in his life, as he was busy with other projects and pursuits. But when he did start writing, he proved himself to be a talented and prolific writer. He wrote articles for various newspapers and magazines on topics such as politics, culture, society, art, technology, and more. He wrote books that were informative and insightful. He wrote books that were creative and captivating. He wrote books that were best-selling and award-winning.

He is most known for his book "How I wrote a million Wikipedia articles", where he shares his experience of being one of the most prolific contributors to the online encyclopedia. He reveals his methods, techniques, strategies, and secrets of writing high-quality articles on any subject in record time. He also discusses the benefits and challenges of being a Wikipedia editor in the age of information overload.

He is also known for his novel "Becoming the man", where he tells the story of a young man who goes through a series of transformations in his life. The novel explores themes such as identity, masculinity, self-discovery, love, loss, and redemption. The novel is based on his journey to becoming who he is today.

Copyright © 2024 Maher Asaad Baker